DESPERADO

ALBUM NOTES

Release Date: April 17, 1973
Top Chart Position: No. 41, reached in 1973
Standout Tracks: "Doolin-Dalton," "Tequila Sunrise," and "Desperado"
Significance: Established Don Henley as a songwriter, co-writing 8 of the album's 11 songs.

Alfred Publishing Co., Inc.
16320 Roscoe Blvd., Suite 100
P.O. Box 10003
Van Nuys, CA 91410-0003
alfred.com

Copyright © MMVI by Alfred Publishing Co., Inc.
All rights reserved. Printed in USA.

ISBN-10: 0-7390-4258-0
ISBN-13: 978-0-7390-4258-8

EAGLES
DESPERADO

CONTENTS

DOOLIN-DALTON 4

TWENTY-ONE 10

OUT OF CONTROL 16

TEQUILA SUNRISE 23

DESPERADO 28

CERTAIN KIND OF FOOL 34

OUTLAW MAN 41

SATURDAY NIGHT 48

BITTER CREEK 53

DOOLIN-DALTON/DESPERADO (REPRISE) 59

"DOOLIN-DALTON INSTRUMENTAL" IS NOT INCLUDED IN THIS COLLECTION BECAUSE OF THE NATURE OF ITS INSTRUMENTATION.

DOOLIN-DALTON

Words and Music by
GLENN FREY, DON HENLEY,
JOHN DAVID SOUTHER
and JACKSON BROWNE

Doolin-Dalton - 6 - 1
25945

© 1973 (Renewed) RED CLOUD MUSIC
All Print Rights Administered by WARNER-TAMERLANE PUBLISHING CORP.
All Rights Reserved

TWENTY-ONE

Words and Music by
BERNIE LEADON

OUT OF CONTROL

Words and Music by
DON HENLEY, GLENN FREY
and TOMMY NIXON

Out of Control - 7 - 1
25945

© 1973 (Renewed) CASS COUNTY MUSIC and RED CLOUD MUSIC
All Print Rights Administered by WARNER-TAMERLANE PUBLISHING CORP.
All Rights Reserved

18

20

DESPERADO

Words and Music by
DON HENLEY and GLENN FREY

Desperado - 6 - 1
25945

© 1973 (Renewed) CASS COUNTY MUSIC and RED CLOUD MUSIC
All Print Rights Administered by WARNER-TAMERLANE PUBLISHING CORP.
All Rights Reserved

32

Desperado - 6 - 5
25945

CERTAIN KIND OF FOOL

Words and Music by
DON HENLEY, GLENN FREY and
RANDY MEISNER

38

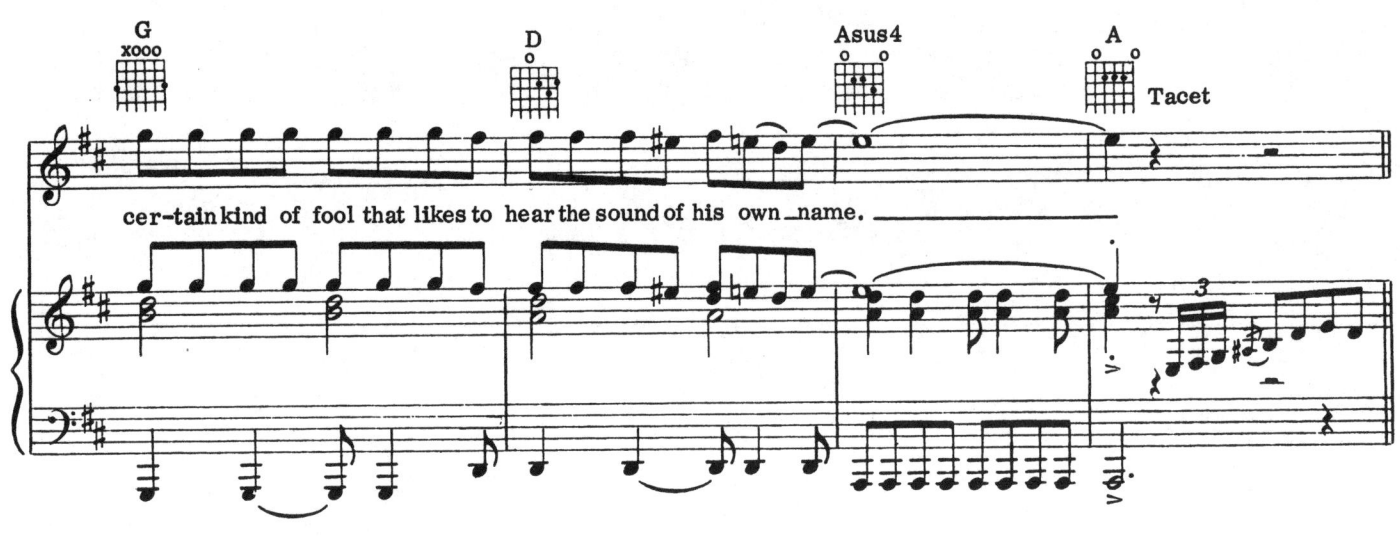

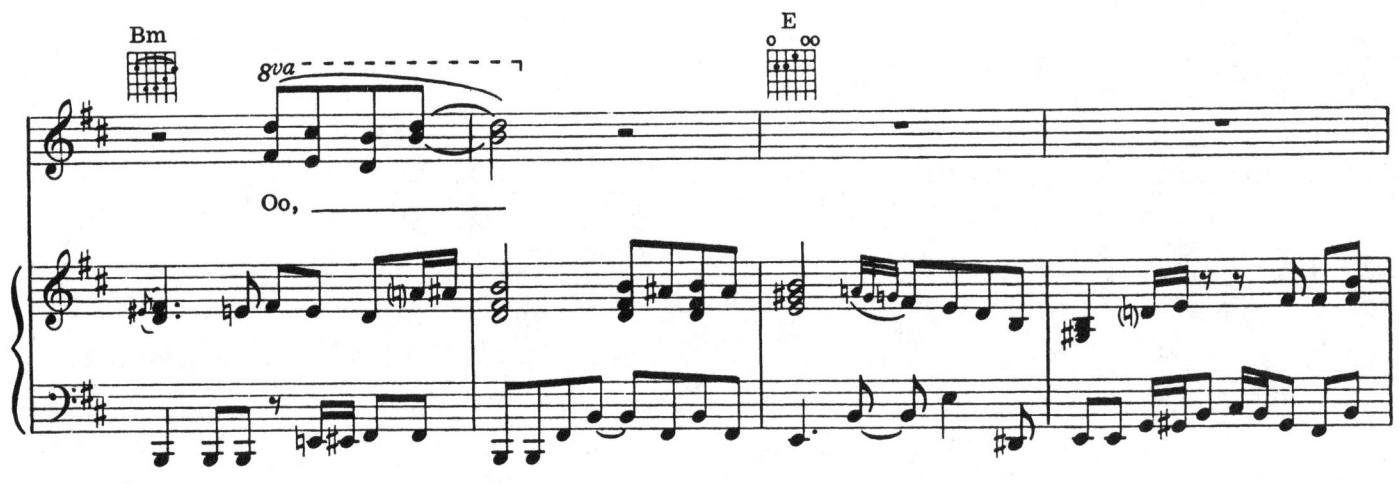

Certain Kind of Fool - 7 - 5
25945

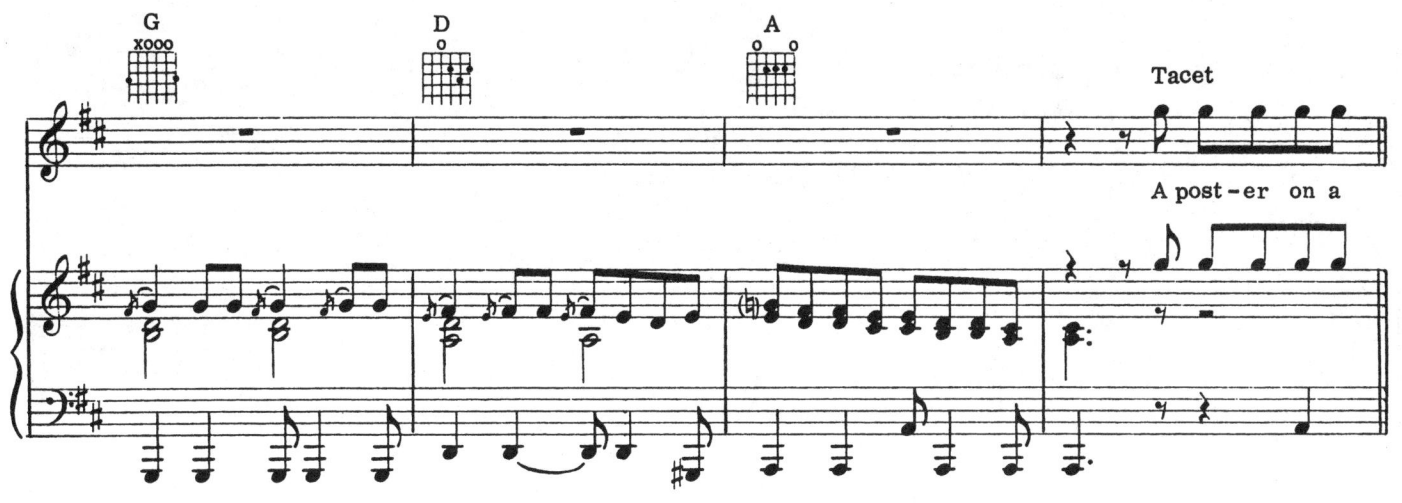
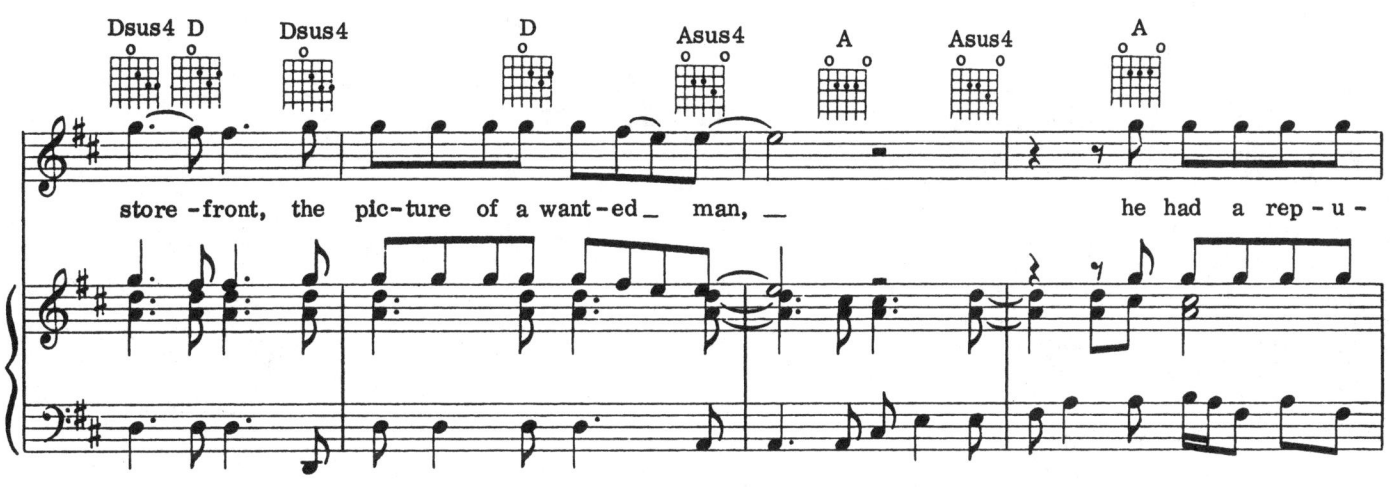
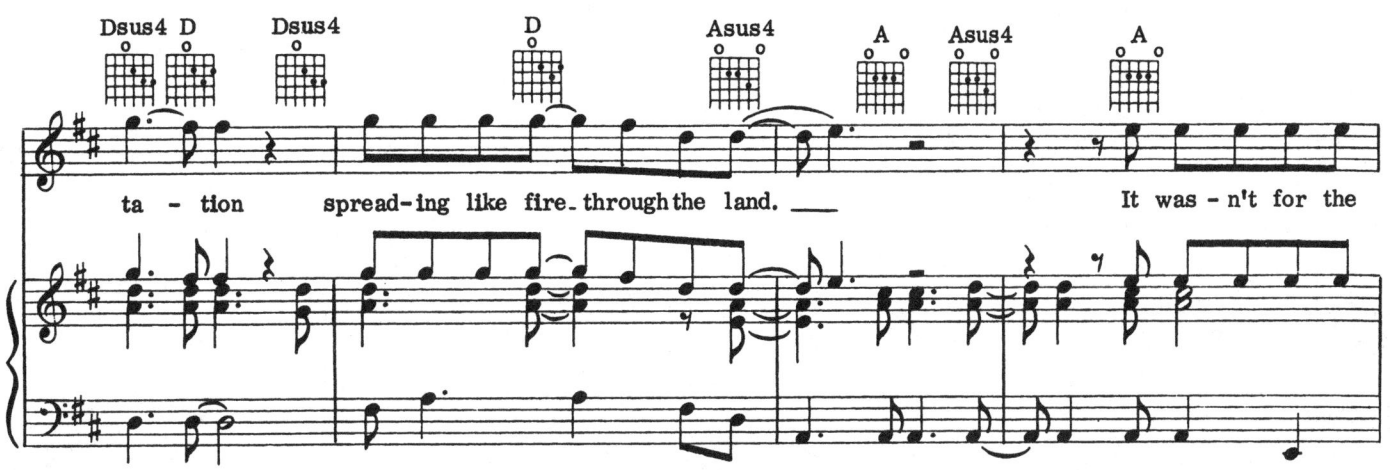

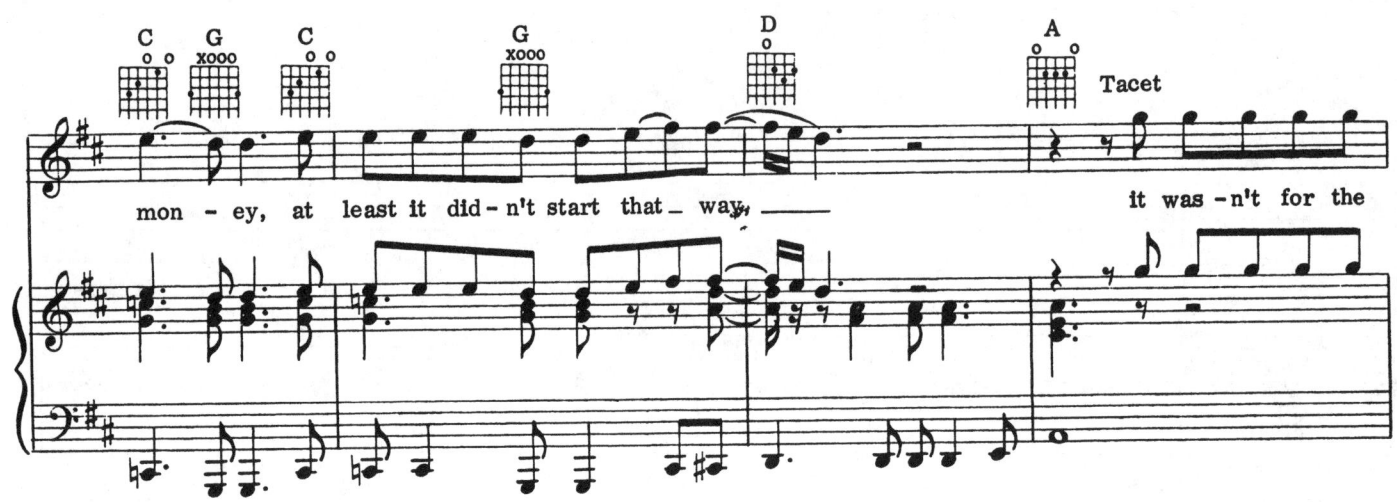
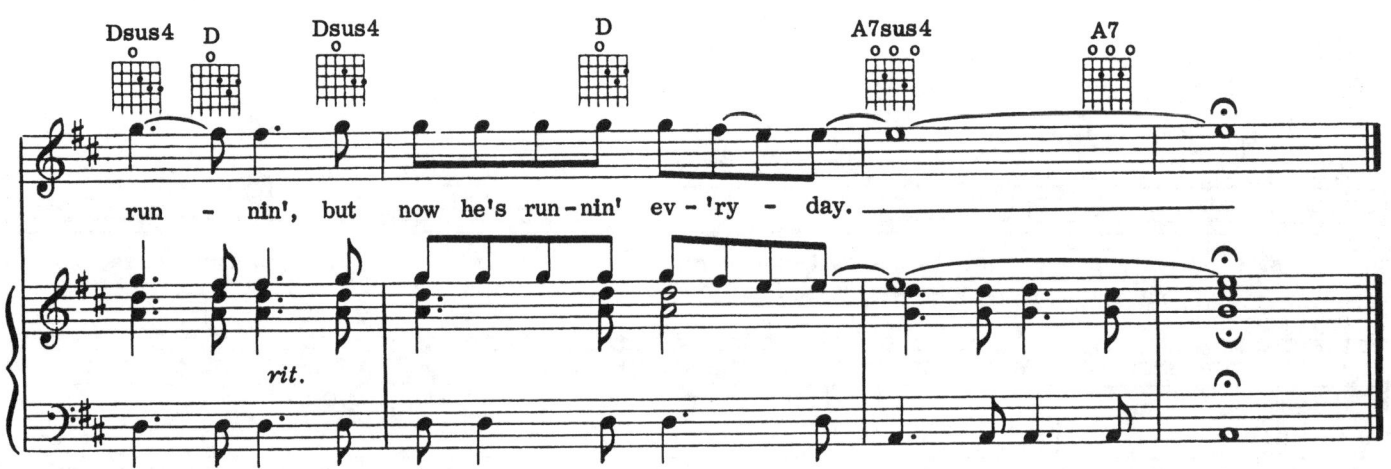

OUTLAW MAN

Words and Music by
DAVID BLUE

44

Outlaw Man - 7 - 4
25945

46

Outlaw Man - 7 - 6
25945

BITTER CREEK

Words and Music by
BERNIE LEADON

56

Bitter Creek - 6 - 4
25945

DOOLIN-DALTON/DESPERADO (REPRISE)

Words and Music by
GLENN FREY, DON HENLEY,
JOHN DAVID SOUTHER and JACKSON BROWNE

Doolin-Dalton/Desperado (Reprise) - 6 - 1
25945

DOOLIN-DALTON
© 1973 (Renewed) RED CLOUD MUSIC
All Print Rights Administered by WARNER-TAMERLANE PUBLISHING CORP.
All Rights Reserved

DESPERADO
© 1973 (Renewed) CASS COUNTY MUSIC and RED CLOUD MUSIC
All Print Rights Administered by WARNER-TAMERLANE PUBLISHING CORP.
All Rights Reserved